MW01027646

THE TRUTH ABOUT
HEALING

An Introduction to

God Wants You Well

Andrew Wommack

Published in partnership between Andrew Wommack Ministries and Harrison House Publishers.

Woodland Park, CO 80863 – Shippensburg, PA 17257

ISBN 13 TP: 978-1-59548-616-5

For Worldwide Distribution, Printed in the USA

1 2 3 4 5 6 / 26 25 24 23

Contents

INTRODUCTION

"Is healing really for everyone? Does sickness glorify God? Maybe it's not God's will to heal me because He's trying to teach me something..." If you've ever asked yourself these questions, you're not alone.

Many Christians seem to think that receiving supernatural healing or living in divine health are out of reach and not always God's will. They depend on doctors, medicine, eating right, and exercise for their health; and prayer, or having faith, is kind of an afterthought. Now, I'm not against doctors, exercise, or eating right; but I believe people have everything backwards. It should be exactly the opposite. We ought to look to God first, but most people don't really know how to start believing the Lord for healing.

Maybe you believe that God *can* heal, and you just throw your prayer out there and hope He answers. If

He does, you think, *Well, praise God!* And if He doesn't, you're left confused, or you give up and think that's it just not His will. I'm telling you, that is not what the Word of God teaches.

In this booklet, I'm going to show you that it *is* God's will for you to be well because He really does *want* you to be! 3 John 1:2 states, "*Beloved, I wish above all things that thou mayest prosper and be in health, even as thy soul prospereth.*" So, it is God's will for you to be in health; and I believe you also have the potential to walk in supernatural health. You can walk in divine health and not get sick. You may be thinking, *That's just not true. You can't live that way.* Well, don't wake me up because that's the way I'm living. I'm going to show from God's Word how you can live that way too!

RESISTANCE TO THE TRUTH

After my encounter with God in 1968, I began immersing myself in God's Word, and I focused on healing. I studied the scriptures on healing and got really strong in that area, and we saw some miraculous things. But I had to renew my mind. It was a process.

Some people came against me for what I was sharing. If you serve the Lord, you are going to face resistance, especially when it comes to ministering things like healing, prosperity, and the goodness of God. Some people just have a religious mindset and won't accept what God's Word has to say about these things. Satan doesn't even have to get involved because people will just do his work for him. Sometimes, I think the devil takes notes when he watches what people are willing to do to resist God.

Years ago, there was a woman who was like a spiritual mother to me. She was really a godly influence in my life and accomplished a lot of good things. But one time, she was visiting with my mother, my sister, my wife, and me, and she started talking about her belief that God sometimes puts sickness on people and even kills them because it's His will. Of course, I countered that by saying healing is a part of the atonement of Jesus Christ. Well, she got mad at me, and we started going back and forth about it.

It was the first time I had ever stood up to this woman. In my heart, I wasn't really mad at her. I was just not willing to compromise on the truths that God had shown me in His Word. So, this lady got mad and left. My mother, sister, and wife rebuked me for it, saying, "How dare you talk to her that way!" And I said, "Look, I didn't mean anything by it, but I'm not going to compromise. God is not the author of sickness, disease, or poverty." But later on, I felt condemned about how I spoke to her. I felt like I shouldn't have done that, and I repented of it.

My oldest son Joshua was just about one year old at that time, and he got sick. I mean, it looked really bad. I was standing and believing for his healing the best I knew how, but I wasn't seeing it happen. I just couldn't figure out what was going on.

Finally, my friend Marshall Townsley came over to our house and rebuked me. (Marshall was my associate pastor in Seagoville, Texas, and he and his wife Cindi were really close to us. After that, they became pastors of a church in

Albuquerque, New Mexico.) He said, "You preach the grace of God—that God is not the one who puts things on you and doesn't punish you with sickness—but you can't live it. You're a hypocrite!" He just blasted me!

Now, I could have just sat there, licking my wounds and feeling sorry for myself after what Marshall said. I could have just thrown up my hands and said, "What's the use?" I could have just opened the door to Satan and let him cause all sorts of destruction in my life, my family, and my ministry. And you probably would have never heard about me if I had done those things.

How I responded in that moment was critical. I thought, *Should I accept what that woman said about how God puts sickness on people and causes them to die? Or should I accept Marshall's rebuke, learn to live out what the Lord had shown me about His grace, about how healing is part of the atonement, and how we could walk in divine health?* (We'll come back to this story later.)

Healing Is God's Will

When I was growing up, my dad was chairman of the deacons in the Baptist church we attended. He loved God and led people to the Lord, but he didn't understand healing. He actually died when I was two years old and was raised from the dead. But he had health problems the rest of his life and died in his early fifties; I was only twelve. My mother was a widow for nearly fifty years.

This happened because our church chose to preach forgiveness of sins as essential and most important, but they never taught about healing. I praise God for all the people who were born again in that church, and that they taught me how to value the Word, but they focused on those things at the expense of healing.

They believed that God *could* heal, but they didn't believe it was His will to heal every time. They certainly didn't understand that they had any authority over healing. The best they would do was just pray and say, "God, if it be Your will."

What I'm about to say may sound harsh to some people, but you're going to stay sick and die if you are not sure it's God's will to heal. Maybe you've been told God wants you to suffer. You may have been told that God put sickness on you because you did something wrong, and that's His way of punishing you. Many people have even been taught that God doesn't heal or perform miracles today. That way of thinking is just wrong, wrong, wrong.

There are all kinds of wrong beliefs out there, but I'm telling you that God wants you well. He has already paid for your healing, and it's up to you to receive it. If you know what God says about healing and plant that Word in your heart, I believe it would be nearly impossible for you to stay sick. I know that's a shock to most people because sickness seems to be the norm, but that is not what the Word of God teaches.

The beginning of how to receive healing from God is believing that it is God's will for you to be well. One of the ways that truth was established in my life was through studying the scriptures. I found out it was part of the atonement. It was part of what Jesus came to do when He reconciled mankind to God at the cross.

Healing is an important part of the Gospel. I know you may have accepted some of the things I've said about the goodness of God and prosperity. But, sad to say, when it comes to healing, there's just a disconnect for some people. You must be willing to accept that healing is part of what Jesus has already done and that healing is available to us.

Now, I know that that's easy to say, and some people may think, *I don't agree with that. God puts sickness on people to keep them humble and teach them things.* Well, some people just don't let the Bible get in the way of what they believe. But if you are willing to listen to God's Word, I believe you will have to come to the conclusion that it is God's will for you to be well!

 "I Wish above All Things"

Beloved, I wish above all things that thou mayest prosper and be in health, even as thy soul prospereth.

3 John 1:2

This was written by the apostle John by the inspiration of the Holy Spirit. What a great truth, and what a great insight into the heart of God. The word *wish* here means that it is His will. God's will is for us to be well. Once we see His will revealed plainly like this in His Word, there's no reason for us to pray "if it be Your will" any longer. Notice that prosperity and health come to us as our souls prosper. We can't really prosper outwardly if we aren't prospering inwardly. Our spirits are already perfect (2 Cor. 5:17 with 1 John 4:17), but our souls only prosper as we renew our minds to what we already have in Christ (Rom. 12:2).

When people are born again, they become totally new creations in their spirits. Their spiritual salvation is complete. They don't need any more faith, joy, or power. They are complete in Him (Col. 2:9–10). However, it is not God's will that we only become changed on the inside. He wants to manifest this salvation in our physical lives also—and that includes healing. This takes place through the renewing of our minds according to God's Word.

And be not conformed to this world: but be ye transformed by the renewing of your mind, that ye may prove what is that good, and acceptable, and perfect, will of God.

Romans 12:2

The Greek word that was translated *"transformed"* here is the word μεταμορφόω (*metamorphoō*), which is where we get the word *metamorphosis*. It's the same word used to describe Jesus' appearance on the Mount of Transfiguration (Matt. 17:2).[1] It describes a complete change. Making our thinking line up with God's Word will also affect this kind of transformation

> We can't really prosper outwardly if we aren't prospering inwardly.

in our lives. Since I was raised in a denomination that taught it wasn't God's will to heal every time, I had to renew my mind to God's Word and transform my thinking to believe it was His will for me to be well. And—thank You, Jesus—that saved my life!

Early in our ministry, Jamie and I were eating dinner with a minister who had preached the message titled, "Satan Is God's Messenger Boy." He taught that God was sovereign and that the devil couldn't do anything except what God allowed, including putting sickness on people. This man told me that I would lapse into a coma and God would use it to break me. I was quite young at the time, and I was willing to accept whatever the Lord wanted to do.

But when that minister also told me the Lord would not allow him to open the Bible or study the Word for seven years, it was like a light turned on inside of me. I thought, *This isn't of God!* Now, I didn't know very much, but I knew this was of the devil. I wasn't having anything to do with someone who thought God told him to fast from reading the Bible! God's Word is His will, and He wants us to renew our minds to it, including where it speaks about healing!

Express Image of the Father

Healing is God's will, and you can know it's the truth because of what Jesus said and did in the Gospels. Let's look at what Jesus had to say about His own ministry:

Then answered Jesus and said unto them, Verily, verily, I say unto you, The Son can do nothing of himself, but what he seeth the Father do: for what things soever he doeth, these also doeth the Son likewise.

John 5:19

Then said Jesus unto them, When ye have lifted up the Son of man, then shall ye know that I am he, *and* that *I do nothing of myself; but as my Father hath taught me, I speak these things. And he that sent me is with me: the Father hath not left me alone; for I do always those things that please him.*

John 8:28–29

For I have not spoken of myself; but the Father which sent me, he gave me a commandment, what I should say, and what I should speak.

John 12:49

Some people have interpreted these verses as Jesus claiming He was less than deity, saying, "I can't do anything of myself." It's actually just the opposite. What He is describing is His complete oneness with God the Father in that the Son could not operate independently of the Father. It's what we call the Trinity: Father, Son, and Holy Spirit. They manifested in three separate ways, but They were one. Jesus also said in John 14:9b, *"he that hath seen me hath seen the Father."* Jesus was talking about the things that He said and did—the way that He operated in God's kind of love.

Hebrews 1:3 says,

[Jesus] being the brightness of his *glory, and the express image of his person, and upholding all things by the word of his power, when he had by himself purged our sins, sat down on the right hand of the Majesty on high.*

Jesus is the express image of the Father's person. That Greek word χαρακτήρ (*charaktēr*), translated here as "express image," is where we get our modern word *character.*[2] Jesus is a perfect representation of the Father, and His character is consistent with the Father. That means everything that is in the Father was expressed through Jesus.

If we look at Jesus' ministry, we can learn what the Father's will is regarding healing. There is not one single instance in the Bible where Jesus refused to heal a person, told someone they hadn't suffered enough, or that God put sickness on them to get glory out of it.

 IS SICKNESS FROM GOD?

But when Jesus knew it, *he withdrew himself from thence: and great multitudes followed him, and* **he healed them all**.

Matthew 12:15

Seventeen times in the Gospels, Jesus healed all the sick people who were present:

- Matthew 4:23–24, 8:16–17, 9:35, 12:15, 14:14, 14:34–36, 15:30–31, 19:2, and 21:14

- Mark 1:32–34, 1:39, and 6:56

- Luke 4:40, 6:17–19, 7:21, 9:11, and 17:12–17

Forty-seven other times, the Gospels show Jesus healing one or two people at a time:

- Matthew 8:1–4, 8:5–13, 8:14–15, 8:28–34, 9:1–8, 9:20–22, 9:23–26, 9:27–31, 9:32–33, 12:10–13, 12:22–23, 15:21–28, 17:14–18, and 20:30–34

- Mark 1:21–28, 1:29–31, 1:40–45, 2:1–12, 3:1–5, 5:1–20, 5:25–34, 5:35–43, 7:24–30, 7:31–37, 8:22–26, 9:14–29, and 10:46–52

- Luke 4:33–37, 4:38–39, 5:12–15, 5:17–26, 6:6–10, 7:1–10, 7:11–17, 8:27–39, 8:43–48, 8:49–56, 9:37–42, 11:14, 13:11–17, 14:1–5, 18:35–43, and 22:51 John 4:46–54, 5:2–15, 9:6–7, and 11:43–44

In light of these scriptures, Jesus' actions are proof enough that it is always God's will to heal. But did Jesus ever actually make anybody sick? If we look through the Gospels, there's not one single example of Jesus making people sick. Yet, there are entire denominations who will still say it's God's will for you to be sick. They'll say, "God

> **Everything that is in the Father was expressed through Jesus.**

did this to humble you, to break you, to bring you to the end of yourself." They'll say sickness is there to teach you something; that it is a blessing, but that's not what we see Jesus doing.

Now, if a person really believed that God put sickness on them because He was trying to work something for good in their life, then they should not go to the doctor or take any medicine. That would be resisting God's plan. They should just let the sickness run its course and get the full benefit of God's correction. Of course, that is not right.

Maybe you're reading this and thinking, *What about the Old Testament instances where God smote people with sickness and plagues?* I'll admit, there are examples of God putting sickness on people in the Old Testament, but it was always a punishment. It was never a blessing; it was part of the curse (Deut. 28:15–46).

> **There's not one single example of Jesus making people sick.**

God used sickness in the Old Testament, but in the New Testament, Jesus bore the curse for us. Galatians 3:13 says,

> *Christ hath redeemed us from the curse of the law, being made a curse for us: for it is written, Cursed is every one that hangeth on a tree.*

Under the New Covenant, God is not punishing any of His children with sickness. The Lord would no more put sickness on a born-again believer than He would make us commit a sin. Both forgiveness of sin and healing are a part of the atonement Jesus provided for us.

Part of the Atonement

There are many people who still don't have confidence God will heal them. It may be that they feel that they don't deserve it, God is punishing them, or they're supposed to learn something. If that's you, I tell you, that way of thinking will keep you from reaching out and just taking your healing. You have to renew your mind to what God's Word says.

Acts 10:38 says that Jesus *"went about doing good, and healing all that were oppressed of the devil; for God was with him."* If that's true, and I believe it is, why would the Father work against Jesus by putting sickness on people? It's

> **God is not punishing any of His children with sickness.**

God's will that we be in health, not sickness; and Jesus is the expression of that will. The sick people who Jesus healed were oppressed of the devil, not God. It was the devil who was causing sickness when Jesus walked on the earth, and it's the same today. Sickness is from the devil, not from God.

> *The thief cometh not, but for to steal, and to kill, and to destroy: I am come that they might have life, and that they might have* it *more abundantly.*
>
> John 10:10

We need to resist sickness and, by faith, submit ourselves to healing, which is from God through the atonement of Christ.

18

Modern-day Christianity has divided what Jesus did through the atonement into different parts, saying that forgiveness of sins is the only thing that applies to every person (1 John 2:2) and everything else is conditional. God may or may not heal you. God may or may not bless you financially. God may or may not give you joy and peace. Many people look at all of those things as optional. But the Bible doesn't say that.

Jesus provided for physical healing as well as forgiveness of sins. The Greek word σῴζω (sōzō), often translated "save," is translated "made whole" in reference to physical healing in Matthew 9:22; Mark 5:34; and Luke 8:48.[3] But the word *sozo* applies to healing. It applies to deliverance. It applies to forgiveness of sins. It applies to everything Jesus made available through the atonement, taking the sins of the whole world into His own body on the cross.

> *[Jesus] bare our sins in his own body on the tree, that we, being dead to sins, should live unto righteousness: by whose stripes ye were healed.*
>
> 1 Peter 2:24

Every sin, sickness, and disease of the entire human race—every deformity, tumor, and perversion—entered into the physical body of the Lord Jesus Christ. That's why His face looked worse than any other person who has ever lived, and His form became so distorted that He didn't even look human (Isa. 52:14). He became sin so we could become the righteousness of God (2 Cor. 5:21), and healing is made available because of the atonement.

James 5:15 says, *"the prayer of faith shall save [sōzō] the sick."* Many scriptures mention the healing of our bodies in conjunction with the forgiveness of our sins (Ps. 103:3; Isa. 53:4–6; and 1 Pet. 2:24). Healing is a part of our salvation just as much as the forgiveness of our sins.

ACCORDING TO GOD'S WILL

And this is the confidence that we have in him, that, if we ask any thing according to his will, he heareth us: and if we know that he hear us, whatsoever we ask, we know that we have the petitions that we desired of him.

1 John 5:14–15

The key to all of this is that you have to pray according to God's will. This has been a stumbling block for some people because they think, *Well, you just can't know the will of God.* They end their prayers with, "Lord, if it be Your will, heal me." That is a total misrepresentation of God's Word.

People will argue, "Well, Jesus prayed and said, 'Lord, if it's Your will, let this cup pass from Me' in the Garden of Gethsemane." That is a misunderstanding of what Jesus said. Some people will think Jesus was saying, "God, I don't know if You want Me to die or if this is what You want Me to do, but if it's Your will, let Me do it some other way." No! That's not what He said.

> **Healing is a part of our salvation just as much as the forgiveness of our sins.**

Jesus said, *"if it be possible, let this cup pass from me: nevertheless not as I will, but as thou* wilt*"* (Matt. 26:39). He knew what God's will was, but He hated the thought of becoming sin and being separated from His Father. He knew that *"with God all things are possible"* (Matt. 19:26), but all the same, He turned right around and said, "Not my will, but your will be done." That was a prayer of submission and commitment to God.

The same Jesus said in Mark 11:24, *"What things soever ye desire, when ye pray, believe that ye receive* them, *and ye shall have* them."* Let me just suggest that you cannot believe you receive your healing when you pray, "If it be Your will..." You have just voided everything.

If you pray according to God's Word, then you can know that you have the petitions that you've desired. For instance, if your body is hurting, say, "Father, I believe it's Your will for me to be well, so I pray, I believe, and I receive right now." After that, even if your body still hurts, but you believed you received when you prayed, that's when you know you have your healing. It's not when you feel all the pain leave or when the doctor verifies it. You believed that you received when you prayed.

The only way you can pray that way—the way that Jesus told us to pray—is if you know it's God's will for you to be healed. When you receive from God, it comes from the spirit first. You receive supernatural healing in the spirit first, and then it comes into your physical body. And you draw that out based on what God's Word—His will—says about it.

The moment you make Jesus your Lord, and He comes into your life, you've got the promise. But that salvation is in your spirit and has to work its way into your flesh. Likewise, healing is made available as part of the atonement, but then it has to come from your spirit into your body. That only happens when you know it's God's will and you believe that you receive it.

Believe You Receive

For verily I say unto you, That whosoever shall say unto this mountain, Be thou removed, and be thou cast into the sea; and shall not doubt in his heart, but shall believe that those things which he saith shall come to pass; he shall have whatsoever he saith.

Mark 11:23

Remember, Jesus said, *"when ye pray, believe that ye receive . . . and ye shall have . . ."* (Mark 11:24). Jesus said that to His disciples right after they saw a fig tree dried up from the roots (v. 20) that He had cursed the day before (v. 14). Although they couldn't see it right away, that tree started dying the moment Jesus commanded it—He believed that He received when he prayed.

When a man brought his son, who was *"lunatick, and sore vexed,"* (Matt. 17:15) to the disciples to "cure him" (v. 16), Jesus used it as an opportunity to teach about belief. The disciples couldn't get the job done, but Jesus cast the devil out of the boy and he *"was cured from that very hour"* (v. 18). Afterward, the disciples came to Jesus and asked why they couldn't do it (v. 19).

If it's God's will to heal, and Jesus healed this boy, why didn't the disciples see him healed? They believed that it was God's will to heal. They knew they had the power to cast these demons out. They had already been given authority to heal the sick and cast out devils (Matt. 10:1, 8).

And Jesus said unto them, <u>Because of your unbelief</u>: for verily I say unto you, If ye have faith as a grain of mustard seed, ye shall say unto this mountain, Remove hence to yonder place; and it shall remove; and nothing shall be impossible unto you.

Matthew 17:20

This is simple, but it's profound. Many people think that if you are believing God, then that automatically means you don't have any unbelief. If you did have any unbelief, then that automatically means that you don't have any faith. So if you were truly in faith, then there would be zero unbelief. But that's not what the Word teaches.

Jesus said, if you *"say unto this mountain, Be thou removed . . . <u>and shall not doubt</u>,"* you will have it. It's understood that you must speak in faith and not doubt in your heart. If being in faith truly meant that you automatically had zero unbelief, then why did Jesus include this part about not doubting in your heart? The truth is, you can believe and have unbelief at the same time.

25

Overcome Unbelief

If we believe it's God's will for everyone to be healed, then why don't we always see every person healed? One of the biggest obstacles to receiving healing and walking in divine health is unbelief.

In Mark's account of this same story, when the father saw his son having a seizure (Mark 9:20–22), he felt exasperated and frustrated. Finally, he looked at Jesus and said, "If you can do anything, help us." He began to doubt and despair. He was looking at the situation and saying, "God, I don't know if You can even handle this." But Jesus said, *"If you [can] believe, all things are possible to him that believeth"* (v. 23). The man's response to Jesus is very telling:

> *And straightway the father of the child cried out, and said with tears, Lord, I believe;* **help thou mine unbelief.**
>
> Mark 9:24

Notice the Lord didn't correct him, rebuke him, or say anything like that. He just turned around and cured the boy. This shows that you can have faith and unbelief at the same time.

Belief is like a team of horses that is hooked up to a wagon. Under normal circumstances, they would have enough power and be able to move that wagon easily. But if you hooked an equal team of horses up to the other side of the wagon and had them pulling at the same time in the opposite direction, the net effect would be zero. Both teams of horses would be pulling on that wagon with all their strength, and it wouldn't move because they're canceling each other out. One team is negating the other. That is what happens with unbelief.

> One of the biggest obstacles to receiving healing and walking in divine health is unbelief.

This is what Jesus was saying in Matthew 17:20. He didn't tell His disciples, "It's because you don't have enough faith." He said, "It's because of your unbelief. Your unbelief canceled out the faith you had." Also notice that Jesus said, *"this kind goeth not out but by prayer and fasting"*

(v. 21). It's traditionally taught that Jesus was referring to the demon who was afflicting this boy. But if you look at the context of what Jesus was teaching, He was saying that fasting and prayer are the only ways of casting out this type of unbelief.

This is the problem I had when my son Joshua was sick. I had faith. I even believed what the Word of God said about healing. I believed it was God's will to heal and that He didn't put sickness on people. Unbelief that comes as a result of ignorance can be done away with by receiving the truth of God's Word (Rom. 10:17 and 2 Pet. 1:4), and that wasn't the issue.

I was in unbelief because I was feeling a sense of guilt and condemnation over the way I acted toward the woman who believed God put sickness on people. I was carnally minded, which leads to death (Rom. 8:6). If I had been spiritually minded—if I had believed what I knew from God's Word, regardless of what anyone else had said—I would have had life and peace.

Cooperate with God

Remember the story of my friend Marshall Townsley: He rebuked me for getting out of faith and not believing what I had been ministering about the grace of God and healing. After he and his wife left our house that day and headed toward home, his wife Cindi got on his case. She said, "How could you speak to Andrew that way after he's prayed for you, helped you, and done all these other things for you?" So, Marshall turned the car around to come back and apologize for being so strong with me. It was only a five-minute trip from their house, but by the time they got back to our house, my son's fever had broken, and he was completely healed. Praise God!

By that time, I realized what had happened. Because my mother, sister, and wife had rebuked me, I felt guilty over the way I had talked to the woman who claimed God put sickness on people. I thought my son not being healed was God's punishment. I had gotten out of faith, thinking that God was refusing to intervene on my behalf. But when

Marshall rebuked me, I saw the truth. I rejected that guilt and condemnation, and my son got healed. Praise God for friends who love you enough to tell you the truth, even when it hurts.

Healing isn't up to God alone. When Joshua got sick, I let guilt and condemnation keep me from receiving what Jesus made available through the atonement. Faith appropriates what God makes available through grace. So, if I believed God was punishing me for something, how was I going to appropriate healing?

God isn't going around putting sickness on people, and He doesn't decide who gets healed and who doesn't. That's a radical statement, but it's true. And herein lies some of the obstacles to receiving God's healing power. One of the worst doctrines in the body of Christ is the belief that God controls everything that happens. There are Christians who believe that God either controls or allows everything, and that Satan has to get His permission before he can do anything (like that minister who said I would slip into a coma and that God would use it to break me).

That's a convenient theology because it absolves the individual of any responsibility. That's also the reason for its popularity! I know this may shock some people, but what I'm about to say is true: that kind of thinking will kill you. God's will doesn't automatically come to pass. We have to believe and cooperate with God to receive what He has provided for us, including our healing.

Healing isn't up to God alone.

One way to build up faith for healing is to learn about others who have received healing. Tens of thousands of people's lives have been affected because of the miracles that we report in this ministry. We have multiple volumes of our *Healing Journeys* DVD series with dozens of testimonies from people who were raised from the dead, or healed of multiple sclerosis, Down syndrome, autism, allergies, brain injuries, and more. Each one of these people had to cooperate with God and appropriate (assign for a particular purpose) by faith what He made available through grace. And in every instance, it required renewing the mind to God's Word.

One of our most popular *Healing Journeys* is the story of Niki Ochenski Weller. Her testimony ministered to millions of people around the world when it was shared through our *Gospel Truth* television program. As a matter of fact, many of the other people in our *Healing Journeys* testimonies point back to Niki as the inspiration for pursuing their own healing.

FAITH IS NOW

On November 15, 2000, I was ministering in the Dallas/Ft. Worth area at the Shepherd's House, where my good friends Rich and Dorothy Van Winkle are pastors. A woman named Chris Ochenski happened to be there that night, and what she heard from the Lord changed the course of her family's lives forever.

Chris' daughter, Niki, was near death due to fibromyalgia and a host of other allergy problems. She was so weak and in constant pain that she couldn't even go to the restroom by herself. She was totally dependent on her parents for everything. Niki's doctor later testified that he didn't expect to see her again because she was that close to death.

Niki and her whole family were fanatical believers. They knew God wasn't punishing them with this terrible sickness. It came as the result of a head injury suffered in a car wreck five years earlier while they were driving home from church. They were believing God for healing, and Niki was very open about telling everyone that she was going to be healed eventually.

However, in my message that night, I said that we shouldn't be *waiting* on God to heal us. According to 1 Peter 2:24, by Jesus' stripes, we *"were healed."* And if we *"were healed,"* that means we *are* healed right now. That means it's misdirected faith for us to just wait on God for healing. We just need to appropriate it. This was totally in opposition to what Niki and her family had been believing.

Chris took home a cassette tape of my message and asked Niki to listen to it. She was blessed but confused about the statements that healing doesn't have to be progressive. Niki previously had a vision where the Lord appeared to her, showed her His stripes and bruises, and told her she would have a progressive healing. After hearing my message and what the Word of God said about healing, she went to the Lord about it. He said her healing was coming progressively because that's what she was believing for—but that was not His best.

Now, the Lord will meet us where our faith is—and that's why some people have progressive healings—but His very best is to receive healing right now.

> ***Now faith is*** *the substance of things hoped for, the evidence of things not seen.*
>
> Hebrews 11:1

Faith must believe that God *is* (Heb. 11:6), not that He was or is going to be. Faith is now! We can aggressively take the authority God has given us and bring healing into manifestation.

I was asked to pray for Niki, so I went to her house the following afternoon. Because of what they saw in the Word about healing and how to appropriate it, Niki's faith and the faith of her parents had been redirected. They were ready to believe for a healing right now! What happened then was an awesome thing. God instantly healed Niki in a very miraculous fashion. Her pain went away instantly, and she was able to live the life God had for her.

Today, Niki is married, has children, and shares about the goodness of God through her own ministry. She has even ministered at our annual Healing is Here conference at Charis Bible College in Woodland Park, Colorado. Praise the Lord!

 # TEACH, PREACH, AND HEAL

Then Peter said, Silver and gold have I none; but such as I have give I thee: In the name of Jesus Christ of Nazareth rise up and walk. And he took him by the right hand, and lifted him up: and immediately his feet and ankle bones received strength.

Acts 3:6–7

Peter saw his mother-in-law healed by Jesus (Luke 4:38) and, like many people, he could have just observed it and moved on. But healing is a part of preaching the Gospel. As a matter of fact, the Lord gave us a command to go out and preach the Gospel and,

Heal the sick, cleanse the lepers, raise the dead, cast out devils: freely ye have received, freely give.

Matthew 10:8

Just like Niki Ochenski Weller, Peter took what he freely received from Jesus (*"such as I have"*) and ministered it to someone else (*"give I thee"*). And because of it, he drew a crowd.

And as the lame man which was healed held Peter and John, all the people ran together unto them in the porch that is called Solomon's, greatly wondering.

Acts 3:11

Healing is like a dinner bell that draws people to God. There are some people who are living in such a hell at this moment, they aren't thinking about eternity in the future. They are just trying to cope with what they are facing today. They aren't thinking spiritually. When they start seeing miraculous healings come, it gets their attention and draws them to Jesus.

> *And Jesus went about all Galilee, teaching in their synagogues, and preaching the gospel of the kingdom, and healing all manner of sickness and all manner of disease among the people. And his fame went throughout all Syria: and they brought unto him all sick people that were taken with divers diseases and torments, and those which were possessed with devils, and those which were lunatick, and those that had the palsy; and he healed them.*

Matthew 4:23–24

Notice that healing the sick and casting out devils were mentioned right along with preaching and teaching. It takes faith on the part of the people receiving the miracles; therefore, our teaching and preaching of the Word is a vital part of seeing miracles. As Mark 16:20 says,

And they went forth, and preached every where, the Lord working with them, *and confirming the word with signs following. Amen.*

Do Greater Works

At one of my meetings, a man who had detached retinas in his eyes asked me to minister to him. Even though I was standing right in front of him, he said I just looked like a blur. With the service about to start, I only had a moment to minister, so I told him to come forward at the end, and one of our prayer ministers would continue the process. He did and, after receiving his healing, gave a great testimony. Not only could he see me clearly, but he could see the faces of the people at the back of the auditorium.

In the same service, a woman came forward whose eyes were clouded with cataracts. She could barely see, but after the prayer minister prayed for her, the white glaze over her eyes was gone. She said her eyesight was great. Another man came off the oxygen tank he had been attached to for months. Deaf ears were opened. Cancers were cured. Backs were healed. Hallelujah!

I want you to know that the most exciting thing to me about these miracles wasn't just that they happened. I was actually more blessed by the fact that I wasn't the one who prayed for most of these people. Years ago, I was the one who was doing all of the ministry. But now, it's prayer ministers we've discipled who are going out and doing good works. Amen!

Don't misunderstand me. I enjoy ministering God's healing to people. But, as the crowds at our events have grown over the years, it has become difficult for me to pray for everyone. I often prayed with people at meetings until after midnight, and yet there were many more who couldn't stay, so they left without personal ministry. Now that we have prayer ministers, hundreds of people can be ministered to each night. Many more miracles are taking place,

> Healing is like a dinner bell that draws people to God.

and it's especially satisfying to see these ministers experience the same and even better results than I do.

Jesus said that believers will lay hands on the sick, and the sick will recover (Mark 16:18). The job of a minister is to train the body of Christ so that they can do the work of the ministry (Eph. 4:11–12). That's discipleship, and that's what Charis Bible College is all about. Now, we're seeing the fruit of that training in our meetings.

Some of the prayer ministers we've trained had never seen a miracle happen through them before. I remember one man who helped us. He received instruction and training; and on the very first night, he saw a person's blind eyes open when he prayed. He told us the next day that he was so excited, he didn't sleep all night. Not only did the blind person get healed, but I can guarantee you, that young man will never be the same. That's awesome!

Whether you're praying for another's healing or receiving your own, it's available to every believer! Jesus gave every believer the power and authority to do the same works that He did. That's quite a statement, but it's absolutely true. John 14:12 says,

> *Verily, verily, I say unto you, He that believeth on me, the works that I do shall he do also; and greater works than these shall he do; because I go .unto my Father.*

The job of a minister is to train the body of Christ so that they can do the work of the ministry.

All believers can do the same works that Jesus did. It's not just limited to ministers like me. With God, all things are possible!

DIVINE HEALTH

God not only wants you to be healed, but I believe that the Lord wants us to walk in supernatural health, every day of our lives. There are a lot of people that take issue with this, but I believe you can reach a place where you stop sickness at the door. You don't have to wait until it gets on the inside of you and then you receive healing. I don't think that's God's best.

Believers who walk in divine health don't even get sick. I believe that's the potential for all of us. And I personally believe that's what God wants all of us to work toward. God wants you well all the time!

Psalm 91 lists a number of benefits for believers, including divine health. It is powerful, and I believe you'll be blessed if you read and meditate on it on a regular basis (Josh. 1:8). It promises a lot of things the average Christian doesn't apply to their life. But I believe it would bless them if they did. If we just take these scriptures and apply them, you can actually use your faith to keep Satan and sickness at bay. Verses 9–10 say,

> *Because thou hast made the LORD,* which is *my refuge,* even *the most High, thy habitation; there shall no evil befall thee, neither shall any plague come nigh thy dwelling.*

Now, what is your dwelling? I don't believe it's just limited to your home. I believe this is talking about your body (but you could also extend it toward your home). This is just saying no plague will come near you. This is a promise for those who dwell *"in the secret place of the most High"* and *"abide under the shadow of the Almighty"* (v. 1).

Notice the word *abide*. This is not referring to the people who visit *"the secret place"* once a week at church. They don't just do a daily devotion. But if you live and dwell in the Lord, every day, all the time, no plague shall come near your dwelling. You will not be afraid of the *"pestilence that walketh in darkness"* (v. 6). These are promises that God has toward us.

There are many Christians who think what I'm talking about is extreme. Some people hear these things and say I'm condemning any person who gets sick or dies, but that's not true. A number of pastors have even come against me on this very issue saying, "Andrew Wommack doesn't believe he can get sick." Now, I'll admit, I'm capable of getting sick,

> All believers can do the same works that Jesus did.

just the same as anybody else. But I've been appropriating these promises and walking in them. And it has been decades since I have had any sickness.

Over the last fifty-plus years, I've only been sick twice. And both of those times came because of my own stupidity. One time, I expended myself ministering almost non-stop without feeding on the Word, so I laid in bed for twenty-four hours. When I got out of bed, I overexerted myself and ended up with a sinus headache. The other time, I worked in a pond in winter, trying to unclog a drain, after going thirty-six hours without sleep, so I ended up with a cold. But that's only two times, praise God!

Redeemed from Sickness

I believe I am redeemed from sickness and disease. And I don't believe I have to have those things. Now, I've had sickness and disease in the past. I've even got a doctor's report that showed I was diagnosed with an incurable disease. And then three days later, I had that same doctor's report proving that I had been healed of it. Praise the Lord!

But I want to encourage you that God not only makes healing available to us when we're sick but, if we would just appropriate it, I believe that we could walk free of sickness. You can walk in divine health. Jesus made more available to us than what many of us have ever experienced, and the sad fact is most of us don't go to the Word of God to find the standard of what we should believe.

God has put the potential on the inside of every one of us that we can walk in divine health so we don't even need divine healing. A person can abide in the Lord and just stay healthy. But we don't start there. It takes renewing the mind to what the Word of God says.

For example, a lot of people think they can only live to the current average lifespan of between seventy and eighty years old. They even point to Psalm 90:10 to prove their point:

> *The days of our years are threescore years and ten; and if by reason of strength* they be *fourscore years, yet* is *their strength labour and sorrow; for it is soon cut off, and we fly away.*

But they don't look elsewhere in the Bible. (It's not good practice to base any belief on one scripture alone!) This wasn't a maximum but a minimum. Moses, the man who wrote Psalm 90:10, also wrote Genesis 6:3:

> *And the LORD said, My spirit shall not always strive with man, for that he also is flesh: yet his days shall be **an hundred and twenty years**.*

You also don't have to be in declining health in your later years. Let's look at what the Bible has to say about Moses himself in Deuteronomy 34:7:

> *And Moses was **an hundred and twenty years** old when he died: his eye was not dim, nor his natural force abated.*

When Jacob met with Pharaoh after reuniting with his son Joseph, he said,

> *The days of the years of my pilgrimage are **an hundred and thirty years** . . . and have not attained unto the days of the years of the life of my fathers. . . .*

> Genesis 47:9

That means people lived even longer than he had! In the end, Jacob lived to be 147 years old (Gen. 47:28). That's awesome!

Exodus 23:25 says, *"And ye shall serve the LORD your God, and he shall bless thy bread, and thy water; and I will take sickness away from the midst of thee."*

The words *take* and *away* in that verse were both translated from the same Hebrew word *cuwr*, which means "to turn off." The fact that this Hebrew word was used before and after the English word "sickness" is saying that the Lord will literally turn off sickness in the midst of us. We can get to the point where we don't get sick.

I'm aware that very few people are at a place for operating in this truth, but it's what's available. It's like running a marathon. Millions of people have proven the human body can run 26.2 miles. You may not be able to do it today, but it is possible to train and work toward that goal. Likewise, you may not be able to walk free of sickness today, but it is what the Lord has made available to every one of us. It should be a goal that we are working toward. That's what Jesus has provided, and I'm headed in that direction because I want everything He's purchased for me.

I don't get sick because I just don't believe in getting sick. I believe divine health has been provided for me and that no plague will come near my dwelling (Ps. 91:10). I believe no germ can touch me and live! This is not something restricted to people in the Bible or "super saints." Walking in divine health and living out the full length of your days is something available to every believer—and that includes you!

CONCLUSION

Second Peter 1:3–4 says God has *"given unto us all things that* pertain *unto life and godliness, through the knowledge of him that hath called us to glory and virtue: whereby are given unto us exceeding great and precious promises."*

Peter was saying that everything we need comes through knowledge. That's because Jesus has already given us everything we could ever need when we became born again (John 1:16 and Col. 2:9–10). Healing has already been deposited on the inside of us, and we just need a revelation of what we already have in Christ. I hope this booklet has helped you understand some of these things—and made you hungry for more!

God wants you healed as much as He wants you to be free from sin. Healing is part of the atonement, and walking in divine health is part of the born-again experience. It's the truth that sets people free.

> *Then said Jesus to those Jews which believed on him, If ye continue in my word,* then *are ye my disciples indeed; And ye shall know the truth, and the truth shall make you free.*

John 8:31–32

This is the truth: God wants you well!

FURTHER STUDY

If you enjoyed this booklet and would like to learn more about some of the things I've shared, I suggest my teachings:

- *God Wants You Well*
- *You've Already Got It!*
- *Healing University* curriculum
- Healing Center resources (**awmi.net/healing**)
- *Living Commentary*

Some of these teachings are available for free at **awmi.net**, or they can be purchased at **awmi.net/store**.

Receive Jesus as Your Savior

Choosing to receive Jesus Christ as your Lord and Savior is the most important decision you'll ever make!

God's Word promises, *"That if thou shalt confess with thy mouth the Lord Jesus, and shalt believe in thine heart that God hath raised him from the dead, thou shalt be saved. For with the heart man believeth unto righteousness; and with the mouth confession is made unto salvation"* (Rom. 10:9–10). *"For whosoever shall call upon the name of the Lord shall be saved"* (Rom. 10:13). By His grace, God has already done everything to provide salvation. Your part is simply to believe and receive.

Pray out loud: "Jesus, I confess that You are my Lord and Savior. I believe in my heart that God raised You from the dead. By faith in Your Word, I receive salvation now. Thank You for saving me."

The very moment you commit your life to Jesus Christ, the truth of His Word instantly comes to pass in your spirit. Now that you're born again, there's a brand-new you!

Please contact us and let us know that you've prayed to receive Jesus as your Savior. We'd like to send you some free materials to help you on your new journey. Call our Helpline: **719-635-1111** (available 24 hours a day, seven days a week) to speak to a staff member who is here to help you understand and grow in your new relationship with the Lord.

Welcome to your new life!

RECEIVE THE HOLY SPIRIT

As His child, your loving heavenly Father wants to give you the supernatural power you need to live a new life. *"For every one that asketh receiveth; and he that seeketh findeth; and to him that knocketh it shall be opened...how much more shall* your *heavenly Father give the Holy Spirit to them that ask him?"* (Luke 11:10–13).

All you have to do is ask, believe, and receive!

Pray this: "Father, I recognize my need for Your power to live a new life. Please fill me with Your Holy Spirit. By faith, I receive it right now. Thank You for baptizing me. Holy Spirit, You are welcome in my life."

Some syllables from a language you don't recognize will rise up from your heart to your mouth (1 Cor. 14:14). As you speak them out loud by faith, you're releasing

God's power from within and building yourself up in the spirit (1 Cor. 14:4). You can do this whenever and wherever you like.

It doesn't really matter whether you felt anything or not when you prayed to receive the Lord and His Spirit. If you believed in your heart that you received, then God's Word promises you did. *"Therefore I say unto you, What things soever ye desire, when ye pray, believe that ye receive them, and ye shall have them"* (Mark 11:24). God always honors His Word—believe it!

We would like to rejoice with you and help you understand more fully what has taken place in your life!

Please contact us to let us know that you've prayed to be filled with the Holy Spirit and to request the book *The New You & the Holy Spirit*. This book will explain in more detail about the benefits of being filled with the Holy Spirit and speaking in tongues. Call our Helpline: **719-635-1111** (available 24 hours a day, seven days a week).

Call for Prayer

If you need prayer for any reason, you can call our Helpline, 24 hours a day, seven days a week at **719-635-1111**. A trained prayer minister will answer your call and pray with you.

Every day, we receive testimonies of healings and other miracles from our Helpline, and we are ministering God's nearly-too-good-to-be-true message of the Gospel to more people than ever. So, I encourage you to call today!

About the Author

Andrew Wommack's life was forever changed the moment he encountered the supernatural love of God on March 23, 1968. As a renowned Bible teacher and author, Andrew has made it his mission to change the way the world sees God.

Andrew's vision is to go as far and deep with the Gospel as possible. His message goes far through the *Gospel Truth* television program, which is available to over half the world's population. The message goes deep through discipleship at Charis Bible College, headquartered in Woodland Park, Colorado. Founded in 1994, Charis has campuses across the United States and around the globe.

Andrew also has an extensive library of teaching materials in print, audio, and video. More than 200,000 hours of free teachings can be accessed at **awmi.net**.

Endnotes

1. *Thayer's Greek Lexicon*, s.v. "μεταμορφόω" ("metamorphoō"), accessed May 31, 2023, https://www.blueletterbible.org/lexicon/g3339/kjv/tr/0-1/.

2. Strong's Definitions, s.v. "χαρακτήρ" ("character"), accessed May 31, 2023, https://www.blueletterbible.org/lexicon/g5481/kjv/tr/0-1/.

3. Strong's Definitions, s.v. "σῴζω" ("sōzō"), accessed May 31, 2023, https://www.blueletterbible.org/lexicon/g4982/kjv/tr/0-1/.

4. Strong's Definitions, s.v. "רוּס" ("çûwr"), accessed July 18, 2023, https://www.blueletterbible.org/lexicon/h5493/kjv/wlc/0-1/.

Contact Information

Andrew Wommack Ministries, Inc.
PO Box 3333
Colorado Springs, CO 80934-3333
info@awmi.net
awmi.net

Helpline: 719-635-1111 (available 24/7)

Charis Bible College
info@charisbiblecollege.org
844-360-9577
CharisBibleCollege.org

For a complete list of our offices, visit
awmi.net/contact-us.

Connect with us on social media.

Andrew's
LIVING COMMENTARY BIBLE SOFTWARE

Andrew Wommack's *Living Commentary* Bible study software is a user-friendly, downloadable program. It's like reading the Bible with Andrew at your side, sharing his revelation with you verse by verse.

Main features:
- Bible study software with a grace-and-faith perspective
- Over 26,000 notes by Andrew on verses from Genesis through Revelation
- *Matthew Henry's Concise Commentary*
- 12 Bible versions
- 2 concordances: *Englishman's Concordance* and *Strong's Concordance*
- 2 dictionaries: *Collaborative International Dictionary* and *Holman's Dictionary*
- Atlas with biblical maps
- Bible and *Living Commentary* statistics
- Quick navigation, including history of verses
- Robust search capabilities (for the Bible and Andrew's notes)
- "Living" (i.e., constantly updated and expanding)
- Ability to create personal notes

Whether you're new to studying the Bible or a seasoned Bible scholar, you'll gain a deeper revelation of the Word from a grace-and-faith perspective.

Purchase Andrew's *Living Commentary* today at **awmi.net/living**, and grow in the Word with Andrew.

Item code: 8350

ANDREW WOMMACK
MINISTRIES

Was Jesus ever
sick???